Water Spirit
A Book of Affirmations

edited by Irene Zahava

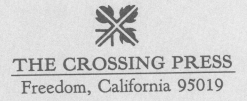

THE CROSSING PRESS
Freedom, California 95019

Other books edited by Irene Zahava:
Moonflower, A Book of Affirmations
Earth Songs, A Book of Affirmations

Copyright © 1988 by The Crossing Press
Cover art by Rowan Silverberg
Interior illustrations by Martha Waters

Printed in the U.S.A.

ISBN 0-89594-257-7

*Free as the
empty
page,
promising
as a full pen...*
—Jesse Cougar

dreams
where you walk the mountain
still as a water-spirit

—AUDRE LORDE

wrap me in the waters
in the silken lilting waters
—NTOZAKE SHANGE

Every woman is an extension of the Earth Mother.
—Yewenode/Twylah Nitsch

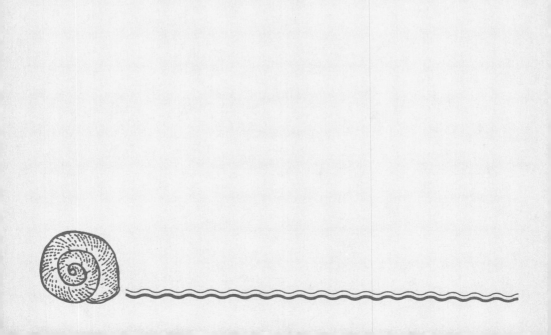

I circle around the boundaries of the earth.
Wearing my long wing feathers as I fly.

— TRADITIONAL

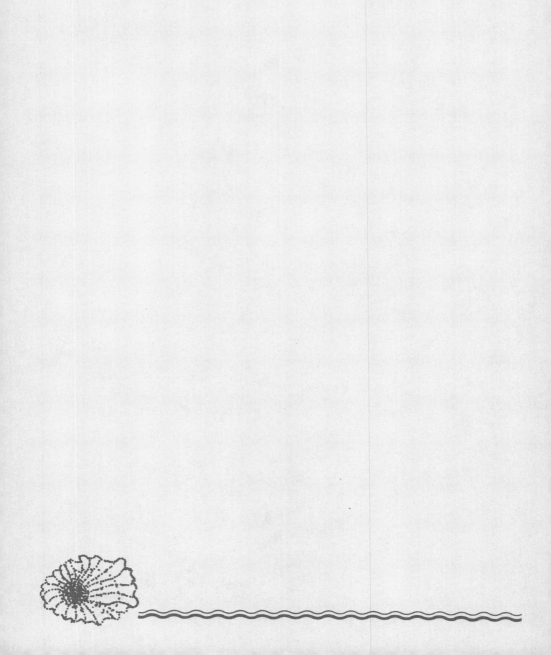

Tonight my dreams will follow the wind
—WU TSAO

the women join
in chant and motion til the hard earth shakes.
—HERTA ROSENBLATT

twilight
taking
the trees
—ANITA VIRGIL

my bare toes
grasp the curving rock:
earth shadow on the moon

—Ruth Yarrow

May you ride the wild winds into the moon's soft embrace.
—Irene Zahava

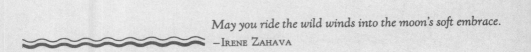

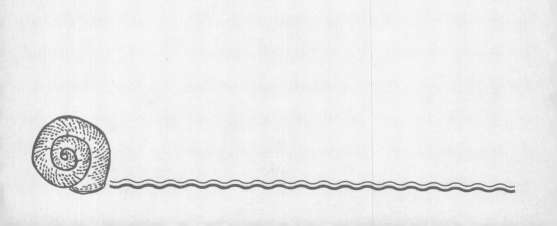

Our spirits
roam the skies the soil & the seas
— NTOZAKE SHANGE

We all come from the Mother
and to her we shall return
like a drop of rain flowing to the ocean.
— TRADITIONAL

The twinkling of a thousand fireflies
the throbbing of our hearts

—Mila D. Aguilar

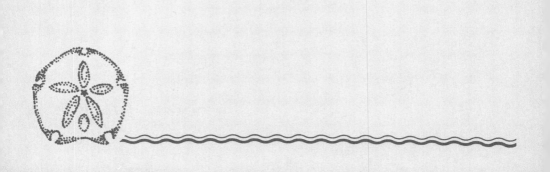

taste me,
  I am the wind
touch me,
  I am the lean gray deer
running on the edge of the rainbow.

—LESLIE MARMON SILKO

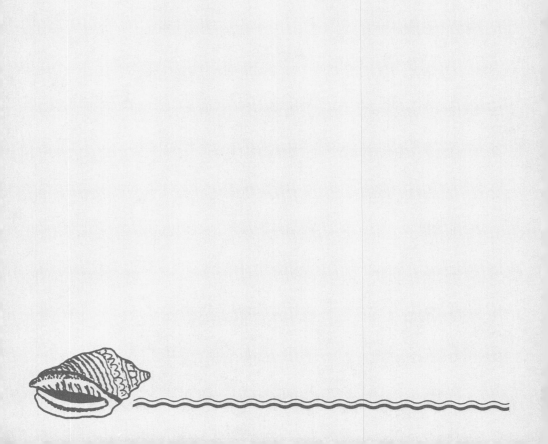

I am the earth, I am the root
—JUDITH WRIGHT

...the skin of the earth is seamless.
The sea cannot be fenced...
—GLORIA ANZALDÚA

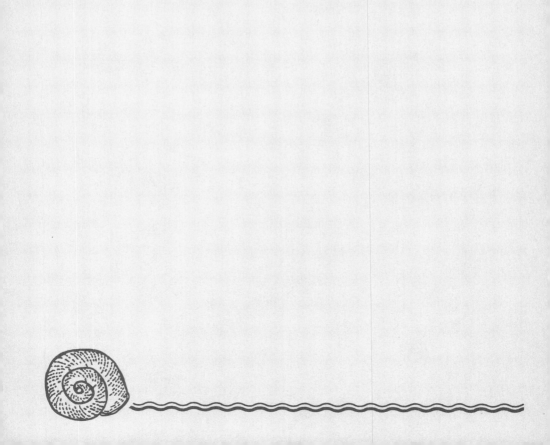

Mother told her secrets to me
When I rode
Low in the pocket
Between her hips.

—MAYA ANGELOU

We consider the artist a special sort of person.
It is more likely that each of us is a special sort of artist.
—ELSA GIDLOW

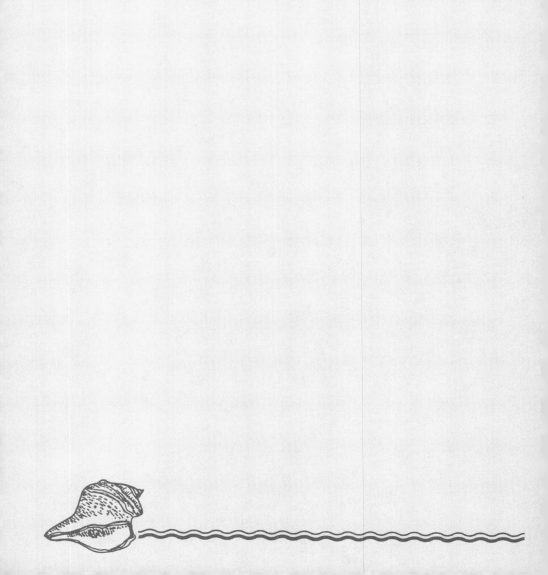

I am the beauty of the green earth
And the white moon amongst the stars
And the mystery of the waters
And the desire in human hearts.

— TRADITIONAL

river silence
magnified by cliffs
and one cricket
—RUTH YARROW

Rainbow is your sister,
she loves you

—LESLIE MARMON SILKO

late sun lays bare
the rosy limbs of the pinetrees.

Sunset in the eternal waves...
—ANNA AKHMATOVA

*the sea will close around what I take out
in cupped hands.*

—SUSANNA STURGIS

I am a dolphin
flowing through the night sea,
the light of the moon sparkles on the waves.

— PEGGY LAGODNY

*Thousands of nights, this round moon has sought
a reflection in the glassy lake.*

—ELIZABETH ERICKSON

*The odor of sea-foam
meets the fog.*

—Judith Mountain Leaf Volborth

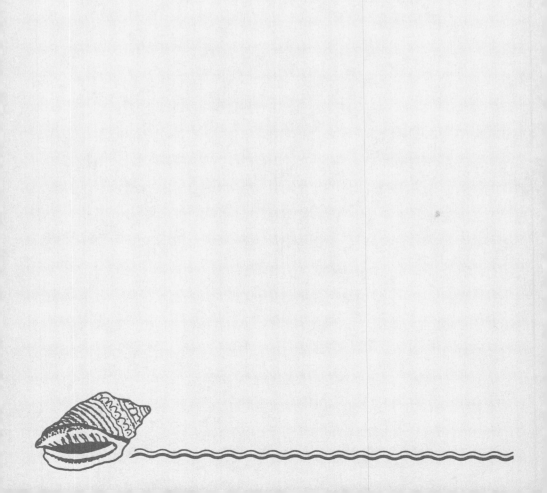

The stars tell stories of the ancient past.
—KAY GARDNER

*This land is the house
we have always lived in.*
—LINDA HOGAN

Some of us, the dreamers, were born to dance upon the wind.
—Traditional

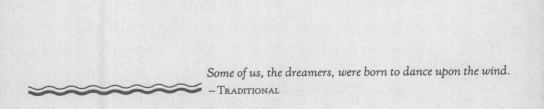

through twilight
the waterfall bends the flood
into sound
—RUTH YARROW

*I dance with thunder.
I like the feel
of rain.*
—SUSANNA STURGIS

The earth is your mother,
she holds you
—LESLIE MARMON SILKO

All night
I heard the small kingdoms breathing
around me...
—MARY OLIVER

As crystal waters dance, the nets are cast,
And soon the moon is caught within the weave.
—KAY GARDNER

Released
from the prism of dreaming
we make peace with the women
we shall never become

— AUDRE LORDE

Rock me in the belly of the Great Mother
Gentle waves surround me
Ocean sing my lullaby

—Irene Zahava

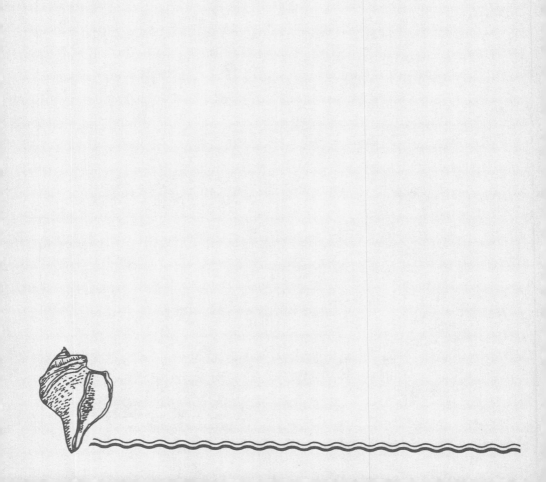

Walking keeps me connected to the earth.
—JUDITH McDANIEL

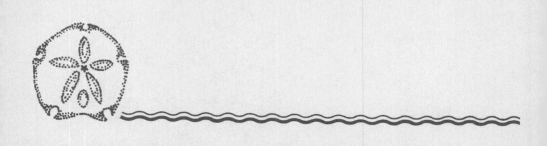

*Mist-filled Moon
rising, rising.*
—Judith Mountain Leaf Volborth

*I heard
a star creak
as it shifted in its galaxy.*
—SHARAN FLYNN TETTLE

The stars above have always been my guides.
—Kay Gardner

At the center of the earth there is a mother.
—SUSAN GRIFFIN

*Sunsets and rainbows, green forest and restive blue seas,
all naturally colored things are my siblings.*

—MAYA ANGELOU

World, I come with my songs;
I come, singing.

          —Elsa Gidlow

skipping a pebble:
black spruces and glittering lake
weave together
— RUTH YARROW

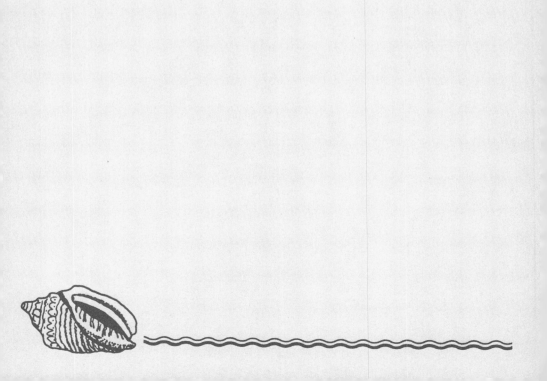

*My strength is
the whole ocean
behind me.*
—JESSE COUGAR

My chant is the beating of my heart...
—Peggy Lagodny

dark trees—dark trees—
weaving their nightdance to the dark wind's melody.
—KIRA MOONSISTER

Strength comes in waves.
—SUSAN GRIFFIN

The sun has set;
the stars, light splinters, fierce and sharp, defy
the dark—the dance goes on...

—Herta Rosenblatt

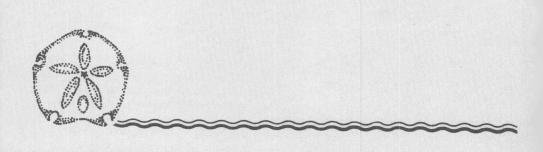

Where there is a woman there is magic.
—NTOZAKE SHANGE

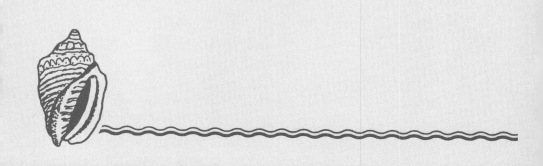

an icicle
drips
farewell
—Yvonne Pepin

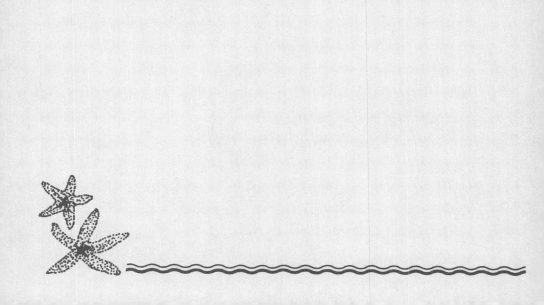

I dream I am precious rock
touching the edge of you
that needs
the moon's loving.

— AUDRE LORDE

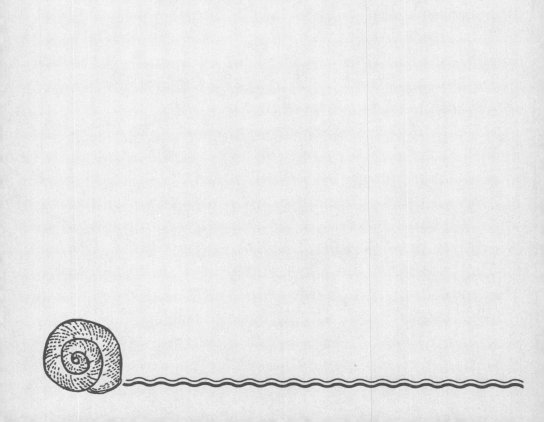

It is the end of August: dancing time.
—Ursula K. Le Guin

*To walk in the city arm in arm with a woman friend...
was just plain essential.*
—GRACE PALEY

*Once upon a time...
there was a womon
and the sea and the
moon.
 Then everything else began...*

—Mau Blossom

After the yellow sunset
The cold moon rises

—WU TSAO

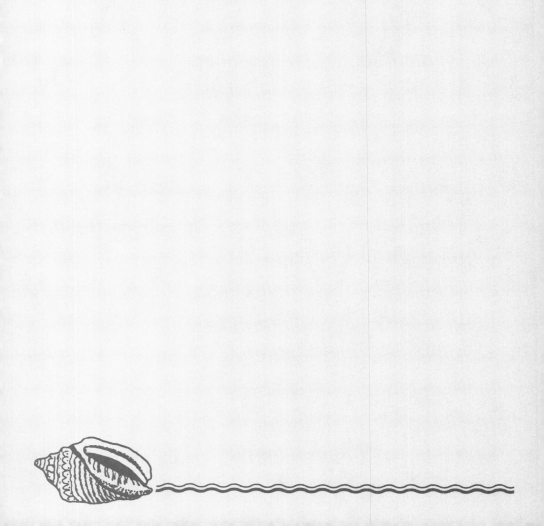

wrap the wind in
beautiful colors / flow like the sea
lie naked in the face of the moon
—NTOZAKE SHANGE

my heart surges to the beat of the sea.
—GLORIA ANZALDÚA

The moon & the sea; they are
—Kay Gardner

*In the dry season we
pull our shallow roots and go
in search of water.*

—Susanna Sturgis

...I know I am made from this earth...
—SUSAN GRIFFIN

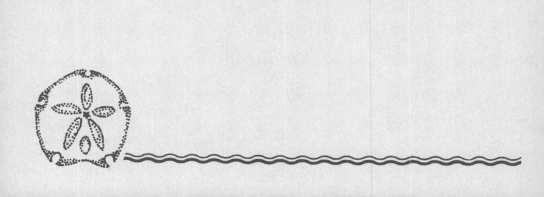

The sea
even by the light of the quarter moon
shines
—MILA D. AGUILAR

*...the love between women is a circle
and is not finished*
    —JUDY GRAHN